Walk Cornw

Helford

CU0040f555

On the path to Pemboa near Gweek

1. Helford & The Meneage
Creeks, woods & quartz pebbles

THE NORTH BANK IS THE SETTING for two famous sub-tropical gardens – **Trebah** and **Glendurgan**. Nearby, at **Grebe** and **Woodlands**, there are two wonderful little beaches. This is a very rural area, heavily wooded and cultivated since at least the Iron Age (800BC–AD43). It's a landscape typical of slate – gently rolling countryside, low cliffs and wooded creeks. The tidal creeks have a secretive and conspiratorial atmosphere best experienced at **Tremayne Quay** and **Frenchman's Creek**. **Helford Village** and **Helford Passage** are the only places on the river that you might describe as 'busy' and even then, it's only really in the summer holidays when the river fills with yachts.

Getting around the Helford by car is not that easy. The road network holds the river in a slightly awkward embrace, either clinging uncomfortably to the riverbank, or madly ascending and descending the steep valley sides. The maze of small lanes give only brief glimpses of the river so perhaps the most pleasurable way to see the river is to pack a picnic, hire a motor boat and chug upriver calling at one of the small quays like **Tremayne** or **Scott's Quay**.

The south bank is known as The Meneage. In Cornish, *Meneage* translates as '*the land of monasteries*'. It was here in the C5th and C6th, just as on the nearby River Fal, Celtic holy men and women set up sanctuaries on the river banks and in the wooded valleys. Many grew into small communities and 600 years after their foundation, into the churches we see today at **Manaccan**, **St Keverne**, **Mawnan**, **Constantine** and **St Anthony**. At **Merther Uny**, above **Gweek** there is a rare survival – an early site that has remained almost unaltered for the last 1,000 years.

GETTING ABOUT
BY FERRY
In the summer, an 'on-demand' foot ferry ❶ connects **Helford Village** to **Helford Passage**. From here you can easily walk to the gardens at Trebah & Glendurgan. Bikes OK. A smaller ferry ❷ connects **St Anthony** to the other side of **Gillan Creek** saving a long walk round.

Ferry pontoon at Helford Passage

BY CAR
The network of small lanes around the Meneage can be a little disorientating – expect to have to do quite a bit of reversing.

BY BUS
Gweek & the famous gardens on the north bank (Trebah, Glendurgan & Carwinion) are served by Helston - Gweek - Falmouth bus (**35**). The Falmouth - Helford bus (**400**) serves Maenporth, Mawnan Smith & the gardens.

Porthallack Beach near Mawnan. The small beaches on the north bank of the Helford are made up of quartz pebbles that sparkle under the water.

Rosemullion Head, Maenporth & Mawnan

A concatenation of coves

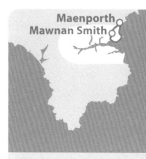

This walk is easily split into shorter sections or could be a single day-long expedition perhaps with a stop for a picnic and swim at one of the many small beaches and coves. **Maenporth** is one of the most popular family beaches around Falmouth – many locals prefer it to the more crowded beaches in the town itself. Of the smaller coves, **Grebe** is particularly lovely. The tiny, pebbly beaches at **Nansidwell** (**Woodlands**), **Prisk Cove**, **Porthallack** and **Cow Beach** are all charming too. At **Parson's Beach** below Mawnan Church you swim straight from the rocks. With the exception of **Grebe**, all these coves are empty even in summer because you do need to walk a while to reach them. You can also take in the nearby sub-tropical gardens at **Trebah** and **Glendurgan** or take the bus directly to Mawnan Smith or Trebah Crossroads, spend a few hours in the gardens, and then walk back to Falmouth along the coast. The bus can be picked up again at Maenporth or Swanpool.

Gatamala Cove

A lovely little beach thought to be named after a wreck here. It's not readily accessible from the landward side so you'll need a boat or to swim round to reach it.

Rosemullion Head

There are wide views across Falmouth Bay from Pendennis Castle south to the Lizard where, as the tide drops, the Manacles reef emerges. The name Manacles comes from the Cornish words *Maen* meaning *rocks* and *eglos* meaning *church* as ships would reckon to stay east of the line between the spire of Mawnan Church and Nare Head to clear the rocks.

BUS

Falmouth (Moor) - Helford service. Maenporth & Mawnan Smith stops. Helston - Falmouth bus via Gweek. Mawnan Smith & gardens stops.

CAR PARKS

At Maenporth, above Grebe Beach at Bosloe plus some spaces near Mawnan Church - they do fill up quickly in the summer. There's room for 5 to 10 cars to park on the roadside at the head of Nansidwell Valley & in Mawnan Smith.

FOOD & DRINKS

Beach Cafe & restaurant at Maenporth, Red Lion at Mawnan Smith. Food shop in Mawnan Smith.

LOOK OUT FOR...

- Swim off the rocks at Parson's beach (a scramble down through the woods)
- The beech woods in Carwinion Valley
- Picnic at Prisk Cove
- Carwinion Garden
  ☎ (01326) 250258

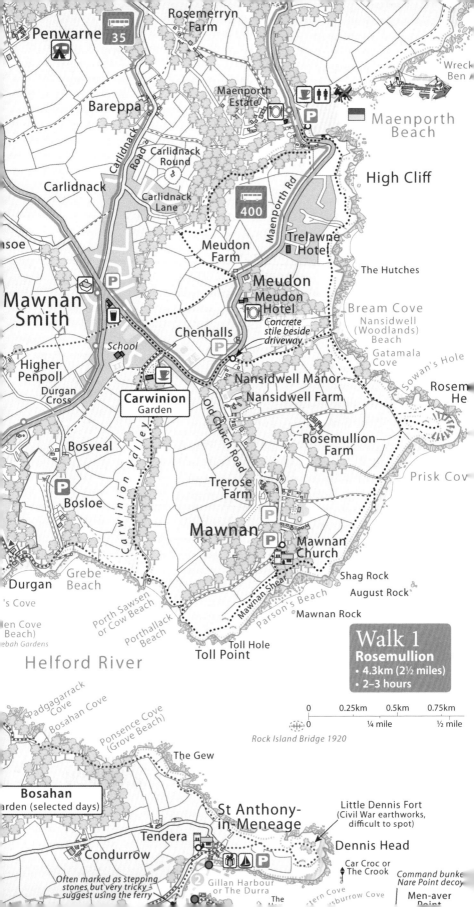

Penwarne

Rosemerryn Farm

🚌 35

Wreck Ben

Bareppa

Carlidnack Road

Maenporth Estate

Maenporth Beach

Carlidnack Round

High Cliff

Carlidnack

Carlidnack Lane

Maenporth Rd

🚌 400

Trelawne Hotel

The Hutches

asoe

Meudon Farm

Meudon

Mawnan Smith

Meudon Hotel

Bream Cove
Nansidwell (Woodlands) Beach

Concrete stile beside driveway

Gatamala Cove

Chenhalls

School

Carwinion Garden

Nansidwell Manor

Nansidwell Farm

Sowan's Hole

Rosem He

Higher Penpoll

Durgan Cross

Old Church Road

Rosemullion Farm

Bosveal

Trerose Farm

Prisk Cov

Bosloe

Carwinion Valley

Mawnan

Durgan

Grebe Beach

Mawnan Church

Shag Rock

August Rock

's Cove

Porth Sawsen or Cow Beach

Mawnan Shear

Parson's Beach

Mawnan Rock

en Cove Beach)
ebah Gardens

Porthallack Beach

Toll Hole
Toll Point

Walk 1
Rosemullion
• 4.3km (2½ miles)
• 2–3 hours

Helford River

Padgagarrack Cove

Bosahan Cove

Ponsence Cove (Grove Beach)

The Gew

| 0 | 0.25km | 0.5km | 0.75km |
| 0 | ¼ mile | ½ mile |

Rock Island Bridge 1920

Bosahan
arden (selected days)

St Anthony-in-Meneage

Little Dennis Fort
(Civil War earthworks, difficult to spot)

Tendera

Condurrow

Often marked as stepping stones but very tricky suggest using the ferry

Gillan Harbour or The Durra

Dennis Head

Car Croc or The Crook

Command bunke Nare Point decoy

Men-aver

Mawnan Church

The church is actually sited within an oval *round* or *fortified farmstead* dating from the later part of the Iron Age (800BC–AD43). They are thought to have been the prehistoric equivalent of the Medieval manor house (*see* Merther Uny & Halliggye). Little, except the oval shape and low bank of the old defensive wall is discernible. It was quite common for the early Christian Church to take over these sites - an assertion of the new political order in the C5th and C6th. St Maunanus, a Breton monk landed in Cornwall sometime in the C6th. The broken cross inside the church is likely to date from the foundation of the site.

Above
Prisk Cove.
Below
The rusting remains of the *Ben Asdale* at Maenporth.

Cow Beach (Porth Sawson or Saxon)

I'm not sure where the name *Cow Beach* came from – *Zowzon* in Cornish means *Saxon* or *Englishman* but I've always know this as Cow Beach. Turn up the wooded Carwinion Valley here to get back to Mawnan Smith. A very pleasant beech wood follows the stream.

The wreck of the Ben Asdale

Just under the low cliff as Maenporth beach comes into view, are the rusting plates of the trawler *Ben Asdale* wrecked here on New Year's Eve 1978. She was supplying the Russian factory ships that were a feature of the time, anchored in Falmouth Bay. Her propeller became fouled in poor weather as she moved away after off-loading her cargo. Despite letting out anchors, she was swept onto the reef here in storm force winds. The ferocity of the storm can be gauged by the way the ship was simply tossed over the 50 metre wide reef and into the base of the cliff. Three crew were drowned, their bodies being washed up at Maenporth on New Year's Day.

Around Helford & The Meneage

Helford Passage, Trebah, Carwinion & Glendurgan

Three sub-tropical gardens

HELFORD FERRY

① An 'on-demand' pedestrian ferry service runs between Helford Point & Helford Passage from Easter to the end of October. Bikes OK.
☎ (01326) 250770

BUS

No bus service to Helford Village but you can catch the Helston - Falmouth bus which will drop you in Mawnan Smith or at the entrance to the gardens (1 hour journey time from Helston). It's a steep walk down to Helford Passage from Trebah Cross.

FOOD & DRINKS

All the gardens have cafes. Pubs – Ferryboat Inn at Helford Passage & Red Lion in Mawnan Smith. Food shop in Mawnan Smith.

LOOK OUT FOR...
- Grebe Beach
- Trebah Garden
  ☎ (01326) 252200
- Glendurgan Garden
  ☎ (01326) 252020
-
- Boat hire Helford Pass.
  ☎ (01326) 250770

Helford Passage is the main hub of the river in the summer. Just sitting on the small beach in front of the popular pub is enjoyable but if you're feeling the call of the sea you can hire a motor boat to explore the little creeks and quays further up the estuary. Children might groan at the thought of visiting gardens but there's actually lots to keep them happy. At **Trebah** paths meander down a sub-tropical valley garden past waterfalls and water gardens and under the enormous leaves of *Gunnera* plants. Visitors to Trebah can also use the private beach at **Polgwidden Cove** for picnics and swimming. At **Carwinion** you can wander through sensory gardens and around the bamboo collection before taking tea on the terrace. **Glendurgan** was created in the early years of the C19th by the Fox family, Quaker merchants and shipping agents. Returning sea captains would bring back seeds for the garden from their travels. There's a laurel maze and an adventure play area. At the bottom of the valley is the pretty little hamlet of **Durgan**, built as a utopian village with a tiny school for local children. If gardens aren't your thing, then **Grebe** is one of the loveliest

small beaches in Cornwall. Or simply walk up through the woods of Carwinion Valley to **Mawnan Smith**, and around to Anna Maria Creek.

0	0.25km	0.5km	0.75km
0		¼ mile	½ mile

Helford Passage

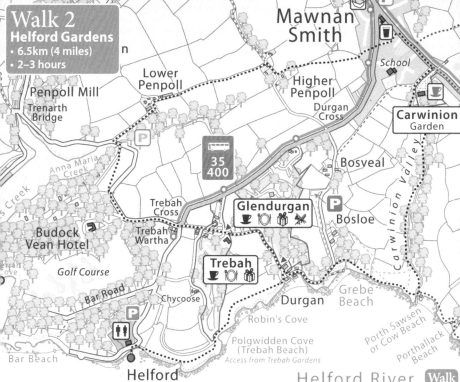

Walk 2
Helford Gardens
- 6.5km (4 miles)
- 2–3 hours

Mawnan Smith

School

Lower Penpoll

Higher Penpoll

Penpoll Mill

Trenarth Bridge

Durgan Cross

Carwinion Garden

35 400

Bosveal

Anna Maria Creek

Trebah Cross

Glendurgan

Bosloe

s Creek

Budock Vean Hotel

Trebah Wartha

Trebah

Carwinion valley

Golf Course

Bar Road

Chycoose

Durgan

Grebe Beach

Bar Beach

Robin's Cove

Polgwidden Cove (Trebah Beach)
Access from Trebah Gardens

Porth Sawsen or Cow Beach

Porthallack Beach

Helford Passage

Helford River

Walk 1

The Pool

Penarvon

Helford Pt

Padgagarrack Wood

Padgagarrack Cove

Walk 3

Constantine & Scott's Quay
Oyster beds & granite quays

Constantine

Gweek

Lizard Point

BUS
Helston - Falmouth bus via Gweek, Constantine or Ponjeravah stops.

PARKING
Constantine has a reasonable sized car park south west of the church. Space for a couple of cars on the roadside at Goongillings.

FOOD & DRINK
Constantine has a food shops & pub. Potager Cafe at High Cross (open Friday to Saturday). Trengilly Wartha Inn at Nancenoy.

LOOK OUT FOR...
- Herons & other waders in the creeks

Scott's Quay is such a peaceful place today, it's difficult to imagine the hubbub that must have surrounded this quay 200 years ago as carts ferried granite and tin ore to waiting sailing ships in Polwheveral Creek.

Goongillings Round
Hundreds of late Iron Age (800BC-AD43) fortified farmsteads or rounds survive in Cornwall – most like this, with their defensive banks incorporated into field walls. You can make out the ditch and earth ramparts on the south and west sides. The east and northern ramparts have been incorporated into the hedge and the ditch has filled in over the centuries. Although the rampart obviously has a defensive purpose (it was probably topped by a wooden palisade), rounds are thought of as more domestic than military places – in the same sort of way that Medieval manor houses could be defended against a small band of raiders. You'll have to use your imagination as there's not a huge amount to see but nearby at Merther Uny (Walk 4) there's a particularly well preserved example.

Scott's Quay
The quay was built at the start of the C19th so that copper and tin ore from Wheal Vyvyan Mine just north of Constantine and dressed granite from the quarries north of Trewardreva could be loaded onto schooners. The ore was off-loaded in Wales for smelting and the ships returned with coal and Welsh slate. Originally, the quay was larger, reaching out to the deep channel in Polwheveral Creek. You can just make out the line of the quay when the tide falls back. The great crash in tin and copper prices around 1860s closed all but the most profitable mines and trade tailed off. Granite export moved to Port Navas where the quays could accommodate larger ships.

Scott's Quay - the line of the original quay is on the right of the figures

Map labels

Comfort
Well Lane
Ponjeravah
Drift Farm

Bowling Grn Rd

35

Site of Iron Age Round

High Cross
Treviades Farm

onstantine

Granite Slate

Little Gilly Wood

Gweal Mellin

Polwartha

engilly Farm

Polwheveral

Trewince

Trewince Stream

Trewince Lane

B

ncenoy

Goongillings Farm

Very steep climb

Merry Meeting

Nancenoy Farm

Site of Iron Age Round

Site of Inow Iron Mine

Port Navas
Inow

Polpenwith Farm

wey

Polpenwith

Scott's Wood

Polwheveral Creek

Walk 3
Scott's Quay
• 4km (2½ miles)
• 2-3 hours

Site of Iron Age Round

owns

Polpenwith Creek

Scott's Quay

Calamansack Wood

Merthen North Wood

North Pill

Lower Calamansack

| 0 | 0.25km | 0.5km | 0.75km | 1km |
| 0 | ¼ mile | | ½ mile | |

Walk 4

Gweek & Merther Uny
At the tide's limit

Helston
Gweek
Lizard Point

BUS
Helston - Falmouth bus via Gweek, jump off at the Gweek stop for the southern part of this walk or, take the Falmouth - Helston bus via the main road (A394) for the northern part of this walk, Trevenen stop. For a longer, one-way walk, jump off at Laity, walk to Seworgan & then follow the stream south to Merther Uny & pick up the bus at Gweek to return to Helston.

PARKING
Very limited in this area. Parking in Gweek during the summer can be tricky. There's some roadside parking at Boskenwyn.

FOOD & DRINK
Gweek & Constantine (1.5km east of Merther Uny) both have a shop & pub. Cafe at The Grange Fruit Farm.

LOOK OUT FOR...
* Tolvan Stone & Merther Uny Round
* The Grange Fruit Farm
* Seal Sanctuary at Gweek

We try to include at least one walk in every book that's off the tourist trail and in Cornwall that often means an inland walk. At Gweek, paths fan out from the head of the estuary, west along a broad valley to **Mellangoose** and **Pemboa**, and north towards the granite uplands of Carnmenellis. In the valleys around **Seworgan** signs of tin mining are everywhere – derelict waterwheels, old chimneys and engine houses. The valley floors have all been turned over in search of stream tin, a naturally graded tin ore washed from the granite bedrock. This area has two of the best, but least known, prehistoric sites in Cornwall. At **Tolvan Cross** there's a prehistoric holed stone and at **Merther Uny** an Iron Age fortified farmstead known as a 'round' which was later reused as an early Christian sanctuary.

Gweek
The Seal Sanctuary brings visitors in the summer but essentially Gweek is a working harbour and has been for at least 2,000 years. In prehistory, the main trading port on the Helford seems to have been further down the river at **Gear Camp** near **Trelowarren**. It probably moved to Gweek during the Romano-British period (AD43–AD410) as the old order was overturned. Large quantities of Roman pottery fragments have been found around the harbour, which led a quiet existence for 800 years or so until Helston's harbour on the River Cober became choked by the shingle of Loe Bar. Then Gweek became the port for Helston, taking on a lucrative trade from local tin mines that only ended 120 years ago. The last great sailing ships that docked in Gweek called here to carry miners and their families to Australia and America in the great emigration that followed the closure of the mines.

The boat yard at Gweek

Tolvan stone

One of the least known but most impressive standing stones in Cornwall is in the back garden of the house at Tolvan Cross and you'll need to knock and ask to see it. Usually these prehistoric stones, which are about 4,000 years old, are simply upright blocks like **Dry Tree Menhir** on **Goonhilly**.

A very few, like the Mên-an-tol in West Penwith, are holed but none are as large as this, which has even had sections cut away in the past to make gateposts. The triangular shape recalls a menhir at Boscawen-noon Farm near Penzance. There are prehistoric barrows in the surrounding fields and you can see one just over the road in the corner of the field – a low mound now no more than half a metre high.

Above
An early (C10th?) granite cross stands within the *lann* or *sacred enclosure* of Merther Uny in its original position near the west entrance (now blocked). Just east & behind this cross are the graves of the Christian community that lived here. Crosses like this probably mark places where outdoor sermons were preached.
Below
Meruny cross in its original setting marking the way to the lann.

Merther Uny

If you're not into prehistory or the Dark Ages you're probably not going to get too excited by Merther Uny. But if you are, this is an outstanding site. You are standing looking at an early Christian sanctuary, at least 1,000 years old, which itself stands within an Iron Age *round* or fortified farmstead which is 1,000 years older still. Excavations in the 1960s revealed C1st BC to C2nd AD pottery and evidence of a timber stockade on the surrounding oval bank. Inside, it would have had all the functions of a farm: two or three thatched round house huts similar in style to those at **Kynance Gate**, stock pens, kennels, perhaps a small shrine, a workshop for toolmaking and possibly a small forge for smelting stream tin to be traded at **Gear Camp**.

Almost all rounds were abandoned in the C5th and C6th when, for reasons not fully understood, numerous settlements moved, often only a few hundred metres, to new sites nearby. Many are still recognisable, marooned in the landscape as oval fields. We've marked some on the maps but there isn't usually much to see. Sometime between the C6th and C10th the abandoned round at Merther Uny was reused as an early Christian *lann* or *sanctuary*. In Cornish *merther* means *saint's grave* and *Uny* is *St Euny* – a well-known West Cornwall saint. It was a small communal settlement with a wooden chapel, the granite cross that still stands today and a graveyard. At some point the chapel was rebuilt in stone, parts of which were later robbed and used in the nearby farm buildings when the site fell into disuse. The nearby churches at **Constantine** and **Mawnan** are also set in abandoned rounds. This site never developed beyond its early stages.

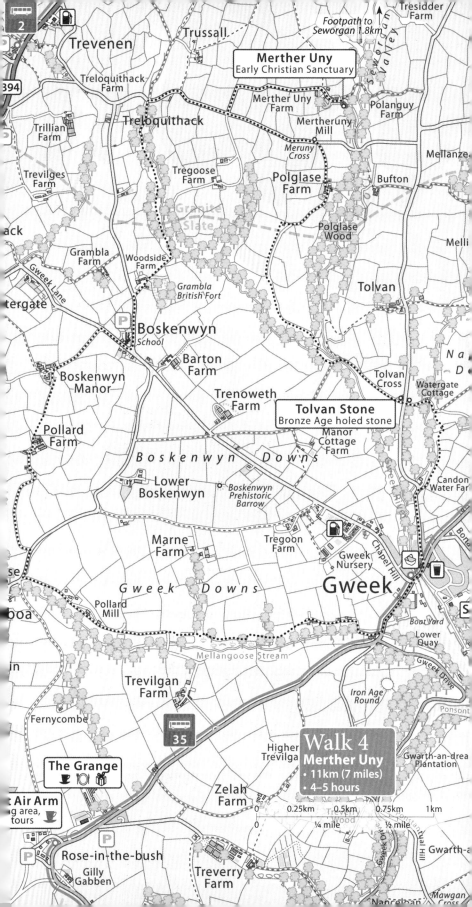

Halliggye fogou.
An underground
passage associated
with an Iron Age
round or fortified
farmstead. Their
function is unknown
– suggestions range
from domestic
(a food store) to
defence or even
religious.

Trelowarren Woods & Halliggye Fogou
Woodland walks, hill forts & a fogou

This attractive landscape, an alternating mix of fields and woodland, has probably changed little since the Iron Age (800BC–AD43). You can see that in the way many Iron Age rounds (fortified farms) have been incorporated into the pattern of fields. At **Halliggye** near **Trelowarren House** there's an example of a round with a fogou – a curious underground passage. At **Gear** there are the impressive earth ramparts of an Iron Age encampment. **Trelowarren House** isn't open to the public but the stables and outhouses are and have been converted into a bistro, gallery and craft shop. Between Easter and the end of September you can park near the house and wander down through the woods and link up with the walk to **Tremayne Quay** on the river.

Gear Camp & Caervallack

Gear's main period of activity was from about 400BC to AD100 but, as with many similar sites, its use seems to stretch back into the Stone Age. These large camps are now thought to be less about military might and more about trade and communal activity, establishing the sort of functions that would later develop in medieval towns – a place for trade, fairs and market days and where disputes could be settled and justice dispensed. Imagine a Roman ship gently slipping into Mawgan Creek, the traders disembarking to be greeted by locals and making their way through the woods to Gear to trade oil, pottery and exotic fruits like grapes and dates for tin collected from the local streams. The enclosure at **Caervallack** is much smaller and more domestic, possibly a residence for the local king or a manor house, a forerunner of Trelowarren. *Time Team* looked at both these sites in Series 9, Episode 7.

Trelowarren woodland walk & Halliggye fogou are only open from 1 Apr to 30 Sept

BUS
Helston - Coverack - St Keverne bus, Garras Methodist Church stop. It's a 2.2km (1¼ mile) walk from here to Trelowarren House but the walk is pleasant, following the drive past Halliggye fogou. You can also pick the bus up at Double Lodges.

CAR PARKS
Plenty of space to park at Trelowarren and there are 4 or 5 spaces next to Halliggye fogou.

FOOD & DRINKS
Ice cream, teas, lunch & dinner available at New Yard Restaurant, Trelowarren. Nearest pubs – Mawgan & Newtown. Spar Shop in Mawgan, farm shop at Gear.

LOOK OUT FOR...
- Halliggye Fogou (take a torch, closes in the bat breeding season)
- Woodland walk followed by tea & cake at Trelowarren

Above
Trelowarren House.
The house isn't open to
the public but the stables
& outhouses are & have
been converted into a
bistro, gallery & craft
shop.
Below
The New Yard Restaurant
at Trelowarren serves
meals, ice creams and
teas.

Halliggye Fogou

Fogous are stone-lined underground passages. *Ogo* is
Cornish for *cave*. They date from the Middle Iron Age
(C4th BC) and this is one of the finest in Cornwall. It's
nearly 40 metres long and unusually well constructed.
Their function is a complete mystery as few objects
have been found inside that might suggest a use.
They do recall the much earlier Bronze Age passage
graves of Scilly and West Cornwall, like Tregiffian
near Lamorna. A ceremonial or religious function
certainly suits the scale and quality of construction
but they don't have the formality of a tomb. There's no
surrounding kerb, or impressive siting in the landscape.
I'm not aware of human remains ever having been
found inside a fogou and also the burial fashion in the
Iron Age was to expose the body to animals and the
elements, allowing it to become defleshed.

Another suggestion is that fogous might be
collective food stores like a prehistoric walk-in cold
room, but you would have thought food would soon
perish in the damp conditions. One thing we do
know is that they always seem to be associated with
settlements. The fogou is often the only part of the
settlement that remains intact – too large and too
difficult to plough down.

Halliggye Farm sits within the original round and
the modern road follows the north eastern quadrant
of the defensive bank and ditch. There's a small creep
passage that opens from the fogou into the ditch. The
only more impressive example is at Carn Euny, west of
Penzance, which forms part of an excavated prehistoric
village so the fogou sits in a more complete context.
The last use of this fogou was as an ammunition dump
for the Home Guard in World War 2.

Seal Sanctuary

Merthen

Bonallack
Cross
Cross

Boat Yard
Lower Quay

Merthen
West Wood

Bonallack Wood

Gweek Drive

Ponsontuel Creek

Helford River

West Pill

Gweek Wood

Gwarth-an-drea Plantation

Bishop's Quay

Walk 7

Vallum Tremayne

Mawgan Creek

Ponstantual Hill

Gwarth-an-drea

Bridge Farm

Gear Hill

Halanoweth

Bunnell

Nanceloan

Churchtown

Mawgan Cross

Gear Bridge

Gear

Farm Shop

Mawgan Bridge

Trelowarren Mill

Gear Camp Iron Age Enclosure

Caervallack Iron Age Hillfort

Cae

Mawgan

Higher Ln

Lower Lane

Carleen

Venton Gannal

Itching Post

Path to Tremayne Quay Round trip from Ten Ton Bridge 6km (3½ miles)

Ten Ton Bridge

Pond Lodge

gan War orial ool

Garras

Halliggye Farm

P

The Mount

P

Trelowarren

Colenso Cottage

Lower Garras Farm

Halliggye Fogou
Iron Age passageway

Gilly Farm

Chybilly

Walk starts from the rear of the car park, or if you want to go in the other direction, walk back down the drive & between the big gateposts

Traboe Schist (recrystallised gabbro)

Chyvarkye

36

Higher Relowa

Walk 5
Trelowarren
• 6.5km (4 miles)
• 2–3 hours

Trelowarren Plantation

Tregac

Exit from Trelowarren only

Lower Relowas

0.25km   0.5km   0.75km   1km
¼ mile   ½ mile

Double Lodges

Beeswing

Trevassack

Dobnas Plantation

B3293

P

Traboe Cumulate

Countybridge

Trevassack Quarry   Countybridge Quarry

Walk 6

Tremayne Quay
Through the woods to the river

BUS
Helston - St Keverne bus. Garras Methodist Church stop & then a 3.5km (2¼ mile) walk through Trelowarren Estate (open 1 Apr–30 Sept).

CAR PARKING
There are 2 or 3 roadside spaces in the valley at the start of this walk but because it's very popular, you can't count on them being free. Plenty of parking at Trelowarren House in the summer.

FOOD & DRINKS
Ice cream, teas, lunch & dinner available at Trelowarren New Yard Restaurant. Nearest pubs – Mawgan & Newtown. Spar Shop in Mawgan, farm shop at Gear.

LOOK OUT FOR...
• This walk is open all year but the Trelowarren woodland walk is only open 1 Apr–30 Sept.
• Arrive on a hired boat from Helford Passage
• Picnic on Tremayne Quay

This lovely walk follows the final part of the driveway that once connected **Trelowarren House** to the river at **Tremayne Quay**. It's a good walk for children; the track is easy going and there's plenty of room for a picnic on the quay itself. They will love exploring the banks of Vallum Tremayne Creek. The National Trust, who own the quay, allows boats to moor here, so arriving on a hired motor boat from Helford Passage or St Anthony is also an option. In the summer you can link up with the woodland walks around Trelowarren.

Great Wood and Merthen Wood have a documented history reaching back almost 1,000 years but they were ancient even then. Oak woodland first spread north from southern Europe as temperatures climbed at the end of the last glacial period 8,000 years ago. What we see here today isn't the wild wood that once reached up onto the downs, the wood that Stone Age man first encountered. As soon as people arrived they started to cut and manage the woodland, making glades to entice prey, cutting trees for coppice poles and harvesting hazel nuts, which were an important part of the Stone Age diet. By the Iron Age, about 3,000 years ago, most of the wild wood had been tamed. What remained probably very much resembled what we see now growing on the poor soils of the valley slopes. We think of ourselves as the great shapers of the landscape, but it was the prehistoric people with their stone axes who tamed the wild wood and had the greatest single impact on the landscape.

Arriving at Tremayne Quay after walking through the woods

Bonallack Wood

Merthen
West Wood

Middle Pill

Merthen
Hole Quay

Tremayne
Quay

Helford River

West Pill

Vallum Tremayne

Little
Wood

Great Wood

Tremayne

Trelea

Bishop's
Quay

Mawgan Creek

Halanoweth

Bunnell

Mudgeon
Farm

Gear Hill

Gear
Bridge

Farm
Shop

Mudgeon
Vean

Mawgan
Bridge

relowarren
Mill

Gear Camp
Iron Age
Enclosure

Gear

P

*Large stone blocks on
the roadside mark the
path to Trelowarren*

Caervallack
Iron Age
Hillfort

Caervallack
Farm

Walk 6
Tremayne Quay
- 4km (2½ miles)
- 1–2 hours

ton
nal

Itching
Post

Ten Ton
Bridge

0   0.25km   0.5km   0.75km   1km

0   ¼ mile   ½ mile

Walk
5

The
Mount

P

Trecoose

St Ma

Walk 7

Frenchman's Creek, Kestle & Helford Village

Conspiratorial creeks (& amorous pirates)

HELFORD FERRY

① An 'on-demand' pedestrian ferry service runs between Helford Passage & Helford Point from Easter to the end of October. Bikes permitted. ☎ (01326) 250770

BUS
There's no bus service on the Helford Village side. The (very) roundabout alternative is to catch the Helston - Gweek - Falmouth bus to the top of Helford Passage Hill on the north side of the river (1 hr journey). Walk down Passage Hill and cross the river by ferry. You'd deserve a medal for that.

CAR PARKING
Large car park at Helford Village & roadside parking for 5 beyond Kestle.

FOOD & DRINKS
Pubs & cafes in Helford Village & Manaccan. Helford Post Office & Manaccan Stores sell food & snacks.

LOOK OUT FOR...
• Kestle Barton Gallery

Frenchman's Creek is famously the setting for Daphne Du Maurier's romantic novel of a swashbuckling French pirate and his love affair with a passionate Cornish lady. Or, as the movie strap line puts it, 'In her elegant world ...a lady of ice: in his world of adventure ...a woman of fire!' – an echo of the duality of the author's own life. The creek is very atmospheric especially early in the morning or the late evening, and like many woodland walks, it's enchanting in the rain. When the tide is out it has some of the eerie ambience of Rebecca. Daphne Du Maurier actually spent her honeymoon moored in the creek having sailed down from Fowey on her wedding day. Foy Vyvyan, who lived at Trelowarren, was a great friend and Du Maurier frequently went to stay. It's a bit difficult to imagine, given how quiet and tranquil the creek is now, that this was once a busy place with three quays serving the local farms. West Quay is used by local fishermen to store nets. Children love running around the woods and paths and there's an old derelict boat hidden away on a tiny beach below the path.

Frenchman's Creek
A memorable novel about a lady and a pirate - their unique romance, their exciting adventures, their strange destiny

Kestle Barton
A beautiful old farm surrounded by orchards. The Meneage is famous for its apples. The path passes right in front of Kestle Barton Gallery which has art shows throughout the year.

Helford Village

Lower Calamansack · Pedn Billy · Bar Beach · Helford Passage · (T) Access · Calamansack House · Boathouse Beach · The Pool · Pengwedhen Wood · Penarvon Cove · Helford Pt · Padgagarrack Wood · Helford River · Treath · Kennels · Walk 8 · West Quay · Site of Iron Age Round · Orchard Lane · Site of Iron Age Round · Frenchman's Creek · Treveador Farm · Helford Village · Bosahan Home Farm · Lodge · Withian Quay · Kestle · Under Wood · Halvose · Slate Breccia · Frenchman's Pill · Manaccan · Meneage Methodist Church · Highlane · Tregonwell Mill · Lannarth Gate Farm · Tregonwell

Walk 7
Frenchman's Creek
- 4km (2½ miles)
- 1–2 hours

0   0.25km   0.5km   0.75km   1km
0   ¼ mile   ½ mile

Walk 8

Around Helford & The Meneage

Helford Village, Manaccan & St Anthony-in-Meneage

Between river & sea

GILLAN CREEK FERRY
② 'On-demand' from the pontoon at St Anthony. Runs 1 April to end Oct.
☎(01326) 231357

BUS
There's no bus service on this side of the Helford.

CAR PARKS
Large car park & loos at Helford Village. Parking in Manaccan is limited to the roadside & can be scarce. St Anthony has a small pay car park behind the church.

FOOD & DRINKS
Shipwright's Arms in Helford, New Inn & South Cafe in Manaccan. Food & snacks at Helford Post Office & Manaccan Stores. Cafes in Helford.

LOOK OUT FOR...
- See the fig tree growing out of the walls of Manaccan Church
- Gillan Creek Ferry & boat hire – Sailaway ☎(01326) 231357
- Bosahan Gardens ☎(01326) 231351

Places where estuaries meet the sea are always full of interest and surprise as they alternate between sheltered creek and cliff. This small area contains three of the most attractive villages in the Meneage – **Helford**, **Manaccan** and **St Anthony** – as well as a trio of little sandy beaches on the banks of the Helford.

Helford Village & Treath

Helford is the largest and prettiest village on the river – a haunt of the rich, the famous and the retired. It's busy in the summer but paths radiate in all directions and the crowds soon melt away. Every inch of the creek is lined with quays and it was once an important harbour. Treath was the original ferry landing place – *'treth'* is Cornish for *ferry* or *landing*. On Good Friday each year people descend to the shores of the river to go *trigging*, in other words collecting cockles and other shellfish. In Cornish *trig* is *ebb tide* and shellfish are sometimes called trig-meat. The river, with its secretive creeks and sparse population, was perfect for smuggling, landing brandy in the isolated coves or by slipping in among the busy trade on the river. The isolated customs house at Kennels was ransacked

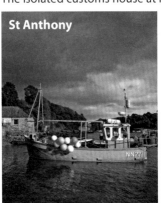

St Anthony

by smugglers in 1840. The excise men had confiscated contraband brandy in Coverack and it was 'reclaimed' by force, but the smugglers did leave a barrel for the customs men as rent.

28

The quays at Helford Village

The Dinas or Dennis Head

A natural place to set up a defence as it commands the entrance to the river (*dinas* is Cornish for *fort*). The first defences are thought to be Iron Age, about 2,500 years ago. This was a great period of fortifying cliffs and promontories and you'll come across cliff castles at Chynhalls and Lankidden south of Coverack. It's probable sites like these would only be occupied in times of trouble. The main prehistoric trade and power centre of the Helford was at Gear Camp and, like many similar important sites, it is discreetly tucked away at the head of a creek well out of sight of any raiders that might sail up the river. As different threats have materialised over the centuries so Dennis Head has been refortified. If it wasn't the Spanish it was the French, and if it wasn't either of them it was the English. During the English Civil War the headland was held for the King to protect the vital revenue from the tin trade.

Below
Little Egrets, once an unusual visitor, are now a common sight on the Helford. Less shy than their cousins the Grey Herons, they can often be seen using their quivering, out-sized feet to dislodge prey from the creek bed.

Above
A fig tree grows from the tower of Manaccan Church.

Below
Looking across The Bar towards St Anthony-in-Meneage. In theory, you can cross the creek here using the stepping stones that are uncovered for about an hour each side of low water. In practice, expect to wade across down stream or, for those who like to travel in style, you can call the ferry that runs from St Anthony in the summer months.

Bosahan Gardens & Cove

A lovely valley garden running down to Bosahan Cove, never crowded. Lots of southern hemisphere plants – azaleas and magnolias are out at Easter and you can wander through palm groves to Bosahan Cove on the river.

St Anthony-in-Meneage

Perhaps only St Just-in-Roseland can match the setting of this riverside hamlet and church. An 'on-demand' ferry runs from the pontoon to the other side of Gillan Creek during the summer for those following the coast path to Nare Point and Porthallow. You can also hire a motor boat, learn to sail dinghies or paddle a kayak up the river. If just the thought of that is too tiring you might simply want to sit on the pontoon with an ice cream. It's an early *lann* church (Cornish: *lann*, an *enclosed cemetery*) probably founded by the Celtic holy men and women of the C5th & C6th who travelled from Ireland and Wales. The farm next to the church is *Lantinning*, so it's possibly the *lann* or monastery of *Intenyn* which changed over the years to the more conventional *Anthony*. There's a small holy well at the back of the churchyard.

Manaccan

This is another early lann church and has a fig tree growing from the wall of the tower. It's been growing there for more than a hundred years and a superstition has grown up around it insisting it shouldn't be harmed or bad luck will come to the village. There is a fine thatched pub, the New Inn, with a beer garden that's perfect for children as well as the popular South Cafe.

Carne

Helford Passage

🎁 🏛 ⛵

Helford River

Helford Pt

Padgagarrack Wood

Padgagarrack Cove

Bosahan Cove

Ponsence Cove (Grove Beach)

The Gew

Treath

Kennels

♿ 🚻

Site of Iron Age Round

Bosahan Garden (selected days)

St Anthony-in-Meneage

Helford Village

Tendera

🚜

🏛 ⚠ 🅿

Condurrow

Gillan Harbour or The Durra

Bosahan Home Farm

Lodge

Often marked as stepping stones but very tricky – suggest using the ferry

The Bar

Flushing Cove

The Herra

Halvose

Trudgwell

Gillan Cove

Breccia

Roscaddon

Gillan Creek

Iron Age Round

Flushing

G

Manaccan

🍴 ☕

Carne Creek

Penpoll Mill

Carne

Tregithey

Tregasso

hlane

🚻

Gillywartha

Little Tregasso

Tregonwell Mill

gonwell

Lannarth Gate Farm

Lannar

Trew

Walk 8
St Anthony
- 7.3km (4½ miles)
- 2–3 hours

0   0.25km   0.5km   0.75km   1km
0   ¼ mile   ½ mile

Walks in this book

	Walk	Distance & Time	Transport
1	**Rosemullion Head**	7.6km (4¾ miles) 2-3 hours	🚌 **Helston–Falmouth bus (35)** Mawnan Smith stop. 🚌 **Falmouth-Helford bus (400)** Old Church Road, Maenporth, Mawnan Smith.
2	**Helford Gardens – Trebah, Carwinion & Glendurgan**	6.5km (4 miles) 2–3 hours via Penpoll	🅞 Helford ferry runs from Helford Village to Helford Passage, Easter to end of October ☎ (01326) 250770. 🚌 **Helston–Falmouth bus (35)** 🚌 **Falmouth-Helford bus (400)** Both buses stop at Mawnan Smith, Trebah & Glendurgan.
3	**Scott's Quay**	4km (2½ miles) 2-3 hours	🚌 **Helston–Falmouth bus (35)** Constantine or Ponjeravah stops.
4	**Gweek & Merther Uny**	11km (7 miles) 4–5 hours	🚌 **Helston–Falmouth bus (35)** Gweek stop at bottom of walk. 🚌 **Helston – Falmouth bus (2)** Trevenen stop on A394 at top of walk.
5	**Trelowarren Woods** *Open 1 April to 30 Sept only*	6.5km (4 miles) 2–3 hours	🚌 **Helston–Lizard Town bus (37)** Nearest stop Garras Methodist Church 2.2km (1¼ miles) walk to Trelowarren along driveway past Halliggye fogou.
6	**Tremayne Quay Stroll**	4km (2½ miles) 1–2 hours	No bus service
7	**Frenchman's Creek Stroll**	4km (2½ miles) 1–2 hours	No bus service
8	**Helford, Manaccan & St Anthony**	7.3km (4½ miles) 2–3 hours	No bus service 🅞 Gillan Creek ferry runs from St Anthony to the Gillan side of Carne Creek in the summer to link with walk to Nare Point & Porthallow. ☎ (01326) 231357